RECRUITMENT, SELECTION AND SEPARATION

GEORGINA MUSEMBI

1

Table of Contents

CHAPTER ONE: INTRODUCTION

Recruitment is an immediate activity between Human Resource Planning and Selection whose primary function is to serve as a link between the two.

The purpose of recruitment is to attract a large group of candidates so that the organization can select the qualified employees it needs.

Definitions:

- According to Beard Well and Holden (1997), recruitment and selection is a process concerned with identifying, attracting and choosing suitable people to meet the organization's Human Resource requirements.

- According to Megginson (1985) recruitment is defined as "referring to searching out and attracting a pool of potential employees from which to select the ones needed to satisfy the organization's Human Resource needs". It involves attracting the right number of people with the ability needed to fill the available jobs.

Significance of the recruitment process

- Enables the organization to obtain the right personnel it needs.

- Enables the organization to improve the hiring standards i.e. selection of appropriate candidates.

- Reduces the cost of training and supervision by getting people with the right qualifications.

- Helps the organization to maintain constant wages and salaries in their wage and salary structure.

- Determining the organizations present and future recruitment needs in conjunction with Human Resource planning and job analysis.

- Increasing pool of qualified job applicants at the minimum cost to the organization.

- Helping to increase the success rate of the subsequent selection process by cutting down on those under and overqualified applicants.

- Helps to reduce the possibility that applicants once recruited and selected will leave the organizations after a short time by providing them sufficient information about the organization thus allowing them to see and make choices themselves.

Factors influencing the need for recruitment

- Growth and expectation (expansion)

- Vacancies created/arising through death, dismissal, the introduction of new technology, etc.

- Mergers and takeovers. As a result of stiff competition in business, some companies may merge to strengthen and maintain their positions. The need for critical skills lacking in the organization for the top position of the organization e.g. General Manager with specific qualifications

- Starting a new organization demands that you employ people.

- Changes in technology and methods of operation. When technology changes there is a need for i.e. training employees and promoting them to it into the system.

- Introduction of new products or services i.e. if a completely new product is introduced in the company and no staff from within it will complete the company to recruit from outside. Alternatively, the existing staff can be retrained.

- Restructuring i.e. organizational restructuring or engineering where job engineering refers to job design i.e. making major policy changes in a particular job e.g. HR director may give a personnel post new meaning as opposed to a personnel manager.

- Government policy on recruitment i.e. affirmative action.

- Nature of the products or services which may have an effect on their demand and which indirectly affects recruitment.

CHAPTER TWO: SOURCES/TYPES OF RECRUITMENT

Internal sources- these include personnel already on the payroll of the organization.

Exter4nal sources- refer to prospective candidates outside the enterprise. They usually include new entrants to the labor force.

Internal sources:

Promotion

- Moving an employee to a higher position carrying higher responsibilities, facilities, status and salaries various positions in an organization are filled up by promotion of existing employees on the basis of merit, seniority or combination.

Transfer

- Change in job assignment. It may involve promotion, demotion or no change in terms of responsibilities or status.

Advantages of Internal source of recruitment

- Familiarity- the organization and its employees are familiar with each other. The organization knows the ability and skills of the likely candidates since they are insiders. Similarly, employees also know about the working conditions and job requirements of the vacancies.

- Better utilization of internal talents- reliance on internal recruitment enables the enterprise make the best use of capabilities of its employees e.g. some employees may be so talented that they deserve a promotion or some may do better when transferred to other jobs.

- Economy- the cost of recruiting internal employees is minimal. The enterprise need not incur any expenditure on informing and inducing its employees to apply.

- Motivational value- internal recruitment is a source of encouragement and motivation for employees. The employees can look for promotions and transfers with hope and thereby do their jobs well so as o earn the desired promotion or transfer.

Limitations of internal recruitment

- Restricted choice- internal recruitment restricts the option and freedom of the enterprise in choosing the most suitable candidate for the vacancy.

- In-breeding- if the enterprise depends too much on internal recruitment it means that the enterprise denies itself fresh talents and new blood available outside.

- Absence of competition- in the absence of competition from qualified candidates from outside employees is likely to expect automatic promotion by seniority and sure prospects.

- Conflict- there may be a chance of conflict or in-fighting among those employees who aspire to be promoted to the available vacancies.

External sources

- Advertising- advertisements in newspapers and periodicals are one of the most important methods of recruitment today.

- Employment agencies- private employment agencies provide a nation-wide or area-wise service and supply.

- Gate hiring- in a country like ours where there is a large number of unemployed people it is usual to find job seekers standing at the factory gates.

- Education institutions- direct recruitment from colleges and universities is prevalent for the recruitment of higher staff in western countries and occasionally in Africa

- Employee recommendation- in order to encourage existing employees some concerns have made the policy to recruit further only from the applicants introduced and recommended by employees or employee unions

- Labor Unions- in many organizations labor unions are regarded as a source from which to recruit manpower

- Leasing To adjust short term fluctuation in personnel needs the possibility of leasing personnel for a specific period may be considered.

- Waiting list- many organizations prepare a waiting list of candidates who have gone through the recruitment process and who have not been employed.

- Field trips- an interview team makes trips to towns and cities know to contain the kinds of employees required by the enterprise.

- Unsolicited applications- one of the important sources of recruitment is unsolicited applicants who send their request for appointment against a vacancy if any.

- Ex-employees- means a person who has even worked in the enterprise and left the organization and now eager to return.

Advantages of External Recruitment

- Provide the company with new and fresh ideas.

- Reduce training expenses by hiring an employee experienced with working at your required level.

- May produce less turmoil and be less upsetting to the current organizational hierarchy.

- Allows for swift growth.

- Can increase the diversity within a company.

- Can make the company more popular on the job market, especially in the current economic conditions.

Potential Disadvantages:

- Takes longer and can cost the company more.

- It can be difficult to tell by the candidate's information whether they will fit in well with the company and its employees.

- Destroys incentive for current employees to aim for promotion, therefore damaging productivity.

- Candidate can take time to become familiar with current systems.

- Current employees may produce conflict over new ideas brought in by the outsider.

CHAPTER THREE: SELECTION

Hiring the best candidate from the pool of applicants, it refers to the process of offering jobs to one or more applicants or candidates from the application received through recruitment.

It is the process of choosing the most suitable candidate from applicants for the various jobs in the organization. It seeks to ensure which applicants will be successful or hired.

Selection methods

There is no single universally accepted selection process followed by all organizations.

The selection process is likely to vary from organization to organization depending upon the nature of jobs and organization.

The following steps involved in the standard selection process:

- Preliminary interview

- Application blank

- Selection Test

- Selection interview

- Reference checks

- Final selection

Preliminary interview

Follows screening of candidates, this is to eliminate unsuitable or unqualified candidates from the selection process.

Application blank

It is the commonest device for getting information from prospective candidates. Most organizations require job seekers to fill up an application.

Selection test

Selection test has been defined differently by different writers and psychologies. Some define it as an objective and standardized measure of a sample behavior.

Selection interview

The next step in the selection process is the employment interview. It is a face-to-face interaction between the interviewee and interviewer.

Reference checks

The reference checks are yet another step in the selection process is used for the purpose of verifying the information and also obtaining feedback on an application the candidate is asked to supply 2 or 3 names of persons i.e. referees who know him or her personality.

Physical examination

The last tool used in selection processes of physical examination the main purpose of conducting physical or medical examination is to have prior knowledge of job requirement with the physical ability of the candidate.

Final selection

It is the last step in the selection process is the final selection of individual candidates for a job having fulfilled the requirements of the job.

CHAPTER FOUR: PLACEMENT

After successfully undergoing through selection process individual candidates are offered employment and place on the job thus placement refers to assignment the right person to specific jobs i.e. relating his or her qualifications with the job requirements.

Types of Tests

All tests can broadly be classified into:

- Ability tests
- Personality tests.

Ability tests include the following:-

- Aptitude test

- Achievement test

- Intelligence

- Judgment

Personality tests:

- Interest test

- Personality test

- Projective test

- Attitude test.

Limitations of tests

- Tests should be used as a supplement rather than as a substitute for any method of selection.

- Tests are better at predicting failure than success. They often determine which applicant will not or cannot perform a job satisfactorily instead of who can or will perform in an effective and efficient manner.

- Tests have no precise measures of one's skills and traits but only sample one's total behavior.

- Tests should be validated in the organization in which these are administered i.e. justify the validity of the test (Degree of accuracy)

- In order to make the Test scores, comparable tests should be administered under standard conditions to all applicants tested for a particular job.

- Tests should be designed, administered, interpreted and evaluated only by trained and competent persons.

- The candidate should be provided with samples of tests or answering questions so as to warm up before the test is administered.

CHAPTER FIVE: SELECTION INTERVIEW

The next step in the selection process is an employment interview. It is a face-to-face interaction between the interviewee and interviewer.

An interview can be defined as an attempt to secure the maximum amount of information from the candidate concerning his/her suitability for the job under consideration.

Limitations of Interview

- Interviews may not have clearly defined techniques developed thus results in a lack of validity in the evaluation of the candidates.

- There is always variation in offering to score to the candidates by the interviewers.

- Interviews can help judge the personality of the candidate but not the disability of the job.

- A single characteristic of the candidates found out on the basis of the interview may affect the judgment of the interviewers on other qualities of the applications (hallo effect).

- The brazenness of the interviewee may affect the objectivity of the interviewer.

- An interview is a time-wasting and expensive device of sample selection.

Guidelines for Effective Interviewing

- The interview should have a definite time schedule known to both the interviewer and interview.

- An interview should be conducted by competent trained and experienced interviewers.

- Interviewers should ensure an element of privacy for an interviewee.

- The interviewer should be supplied with a specific set of guidelines for conducting the interview.

- The resume/summary for the entire candidate to be interviewed should be prepared

- The interview should not end abruptly but it should come to a close tactfully providing satisfaction to the interviewee.

- Interviewers should show their sensitivity to the interviews sentiments and also a sympathetic attitude to him/her.

- Interviewers should also show emotional maturity and stable emotionality during interview time.

Benefits of good placement

- Reduces employee turnover.

- Reduces absenteeism.

- Reduces accident rates

- Improves morale and commitment

- Improves performance and productivity

- Reduces the cost of operation

- Improves career growth and development i.e. individual remains focused on a particular career.

- Reduces work related conflicts and grievances

- Reduces employee stress

CHAPTER SIX: INDUCTION / ORIENTATION

Induction is the process through which new employees are introduced to the job and the entire organization.

Objectives of the Induction Programme

- To introduce new employees to the organization's work procedures, rules, and regulations

- To familiarize employees with the work environment, fellow workmates, immediate supervisor, and departmental head

- To set new employees at ease in their new jobs and instill confidence

- Reduce fears and anxiety associated with work in a new environment such as feelings of insecurity and nervousness

- To explain to new employees duties and responsibilities and introduce the person to report to when he has a problem

- To introduce new employees to general employment conditions of the organization i.e. organizational policies and procedures

Areas covered by an induction programme

- The significance of the job with all necessary information about it including job training and hazards

- The company, its history, products or services, the process of production and major activities involved in an individual work

- Structure of the organization i.e. the geographical location of the plan and the faction of various departments.

- Employee's department and how such department fits in the organization

- The relationship between employee's departments and other departments

- Company policies, practices, and procedures

- Terms and conditions of service including the welfare services

- Rules and regulations governing hours of work, over time, safety accident prevention, holidays, etc.

- Social benefits, insurance and pension scheme, etc.

- Opportunities for promotions and transfers

Benefits of Induction

- Improves confidence in the job hence productivity/performance of the employee is increased.

- Improves employee relationship which results in team spirit in the organization

- Helps organizations reduce the cost of operation i.e. an employee does not waste/spend unnecessary time doing personal work.

- Reduces the rate of labor turnover in an organization due to job frustration

- Reduces on-the-job training cost as well as off-the-job training in future

- Promotes loyalty and commitment to the organization

- Improves the relationship between employees and their bosses

- Improves safety measures which reduce industrial accidents

CHAPTER SEVEN: SEPARATION

If the first function of Human Resource Management is to acquire an employee then it follows that the last function is separation. It occurs when the employment relationship is terminated and the employee leaves the organization

The decisions can be initiated by the employer as well as the employee. These may be retirements, retrenchment, resignation, discharge, dismissal, and death

- Retirements

Retirement is stopping to work after attaining a predetermined age as the employee can no longer maintain the pace or is not willing to work anymore. Various occupations have different retirement methods, in all organizations, there must be stipulated retirement regulations. Since retirement is an important stage in an employee's life, the company has an important role to play in this transition

It is an important opportunity for them to make decisions on their personal and social lives. It's the responsibility of the employer to make retirement plans for employee and also educate them on how to plan for retirement and spend the period. Many organizations have retirement benefits for their employees some include holidays, pension benefits and other retirement packages

Some companies have mandatory social security fund contributions while others have insurance company's pension schemes.

Mandatory retirement benefits

- It's simple to administer

- It creates an opportunity for younger employees to exploit their potential

- It aids human resource forecasts and plans

- It enables employees to plan for their exit well in advance

- Reduces inequities in decision making in regard to separation

Resignation

This is a voluntary termination of employment contract by an employee. It is also known as voluntary employee turnover

It occurs for a variety of reasons:

- New and better employment offers elsewhere

- Joining a spouse and other family obligations

- Ill-health

- Poor working conditions

- Poor management

Retirement should be avoided at all costs as it places a heavy burden on a company due to hiring costs, training costs, overtime costs. However, sometimes it's good because it helps to cushion the company against impending redundancies.

An appointment may be terminated by one party giving the other a one month notice in writing or by paying one month's gross salary in lieu of notice. Some permanent and pensionable jobs require a three-month notice. Employees should exit peacefully without causing resentment.

Dismissals

This occurs when an employee's job is terminated by the employer due to poor productivity or indiscipline. This is also referred to as summary dismissal and is a very painful method of separation. It is usually a traumatic experience because employees suffer shattered egos.

An employee can be dismissed on the following grounds:

- Absents from work without leave

- Financial embezzlement

- Unable to perform duties due to drunkenness or intoxication

- Wilfully neglects to perform assigned tasks or performs them carelessly

- Uses abusive or insulting language

- Arrested for an offense punishable by imprisonment

- Commits an offense against an employer

However, employees are protected against unfair dismissals through union/management agreements.

Death

This occurs when an employee dies while still working for an organization. It is known as natural attrition this may be due to accidents in and outside of duty, illness, etc. Though it's inevitable it leads to a great economic and social loss to organizations, families, and friends. It's important that organizations put in place mechanisms such as good health and counseling programmes which will ensure the good continued physical and mental health of employees

Chronic illnesses are causing fatalities at the place of work e.g. Cancer, HBP, AIDS, etc. death can no longer be seen just like natural attrition but a major decimator of the entire workforce and work skills. Human Resource managers must plan to counteract the effects of high mortality rates among the workforce occasioned by the disease.

- Redundancy

It is any situation where changes in the organizations economic, operational, or technological position result in reduced demand for manpower. It has been variously referred to as layoffs, downsizing, rightsizing, reduction in force or retrenchment, downsizing, excess reduction, rightsizing, delayering, smartsizing, redeployment, workforce reduction, workforce optimization, simplification, force shaping, and reduction in force

It's the most painful exercises which Human Resource Management have to deal with because it involves an abrupt loss of earnings, separation from colleagues, loss of personality and many uncertainties. It's therefore imperative that in case of an imminent redundancy where a company is unionized, must consult the relevant trade union well in advance about an impending redundancy

Types of redundancies

- Job Redundancy

This occurs when a particular job ceases to exist but the incident employees are assigned alternative work or job within the organization

- Worker redundancy

Occurs when employees lose their employment because of overstaffing i.e. very little work being done by too many people

Measures used to minimize problems of redundancy

- Planning ahead

It's important for the HRM to plan for reduced staff needs in the future. With proper HR forecasts and plans the future reduction in staff needs can be cushioned through natural attrition, reducing or freezing recruitment of new staff, etc.

- Voluntary retirement

This is a method which is used for enticing employees to terminate their services with a handsome pay-off or golden handshake or premium. For employees to be persuaded to leave, the offer must be well above the statutory rates

- Applying contingency plans

i. Terminating part time service

ii. Eliminating overtime

iii. Removal of out-sourced contracts

iv. Job sharing

v. Applying temporary lay-offs

- Outplacement

This is where redundant employees are assisted in finding alternative employment elsewhere. For outplacement to be beneficial there is a need for counseling programmes which help the employee to fit into new careers more effectively

Handling redundancies

When circumstances force management to lay-off employees, its imperative that redundancy procedures adapted are fair and equitable for all employees

They may occur due to:

- Increase in the level of economic activity eg. Competition may lead to a decline in demand for the products.

- Introduction of technological changes

- The re-organization of the work situation

- Shortage of raw materials/equipment components which affect the ability to produce

- Mergers or relocation of the organizations

- Changes in seasons of service or production

Redundancy selection criteria

It's important that the management sets criteria, which will be applied either across ALL or PARTS of its labor force. If redundancy is applied across ALL organizations, it means all departments and all levels in the hierarchy will be affected. When applied to a PART of the labor force, it will only affect certain departments and types of employees

- Last in first out

This is the most used and the one favored by trade unions. The principle is that the longer the employee has been with an organization, the greater their right to a job and therefore redundant employees should be selected on the basis of their length of service. By using the seniority of service, it avoids favoritism and discrimination. In this way, the organization retains an employee who has a long service and possesses the required skills or experience

- Efficiency

Many organizations select their redundant employees from among those who show poor work performance, habitual absenteeism, lateness, or any other form of indiscipline. However, trade unions tend to resist this approach unless they have been provided with prior information showing that such shortcomings really exist

- Qualifications and flexibility

Depends on how an employee is more qualified or multi-skilled than the other. Less qualified employees are the one normally selected for redundancy

- Age

The older an employee is, the more easily he/she will be selected for redundancy than the younger employees.

- Special cases

The more knowledgeable and expert an employee is, the less likely is he/she to be selected for redundancy and vice versa

Other methods of separation

- Termination on medical grounds

- Termination during probation.

- Layoff

- Normal termination